MATH
ACTIVITY BOOK
For Kids

This Book Belongs To

_____

_____

_____

Belongs to page

- Trace and write the number
- Number count and write
- Put the correct number in the box
- Missing number
- Number maze
- Adding number
- Adding worksheet matching
- Write the number in the box
- Subtraction
- Addition with object
- Subtraction with object
- Circle the number with picture

Trace and Write with the word

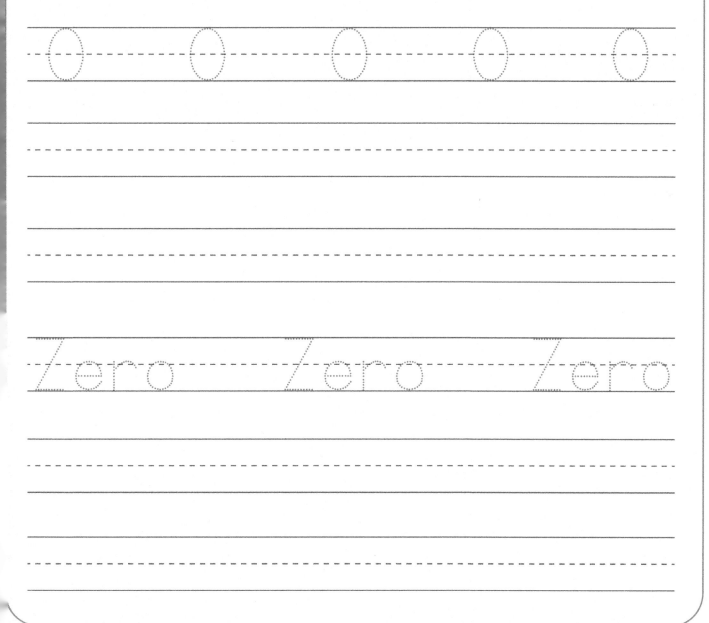

Trace and Write with the word

One   One   One

Trace and Write with the word

3 - - - 3 - - - 3 - - - 3 - - - 3

Three - Three - Three

4 4 4 4 4

four   four   four

Trace and Write with the word

7 7 7 7 7

Seven Seven Seven

9   9   9   9   9

Nine   Nine   Nine

Let's Learn the number Count and Write

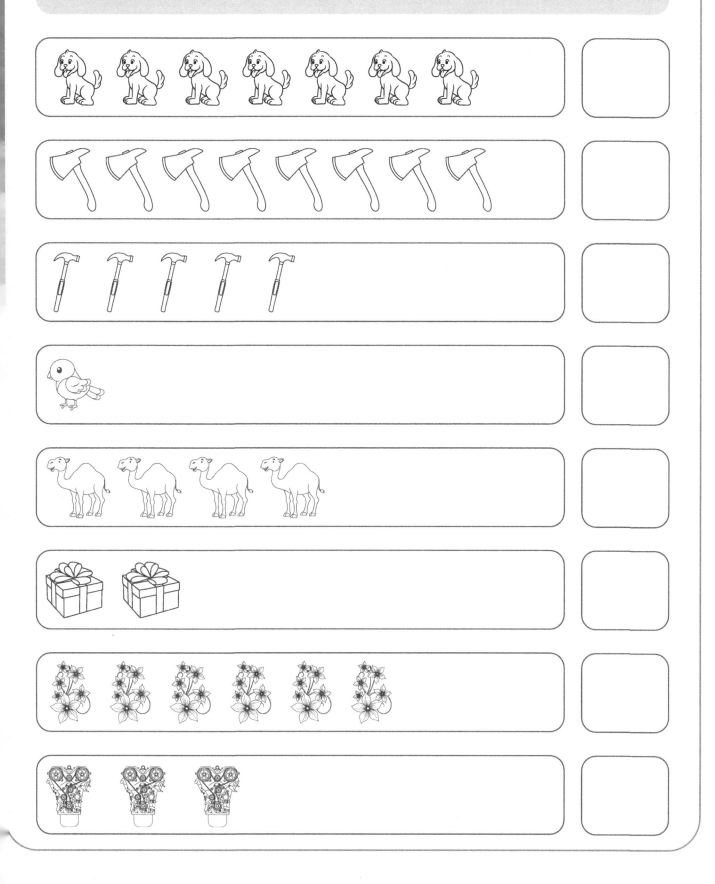

Let's Learn the number Count and Write

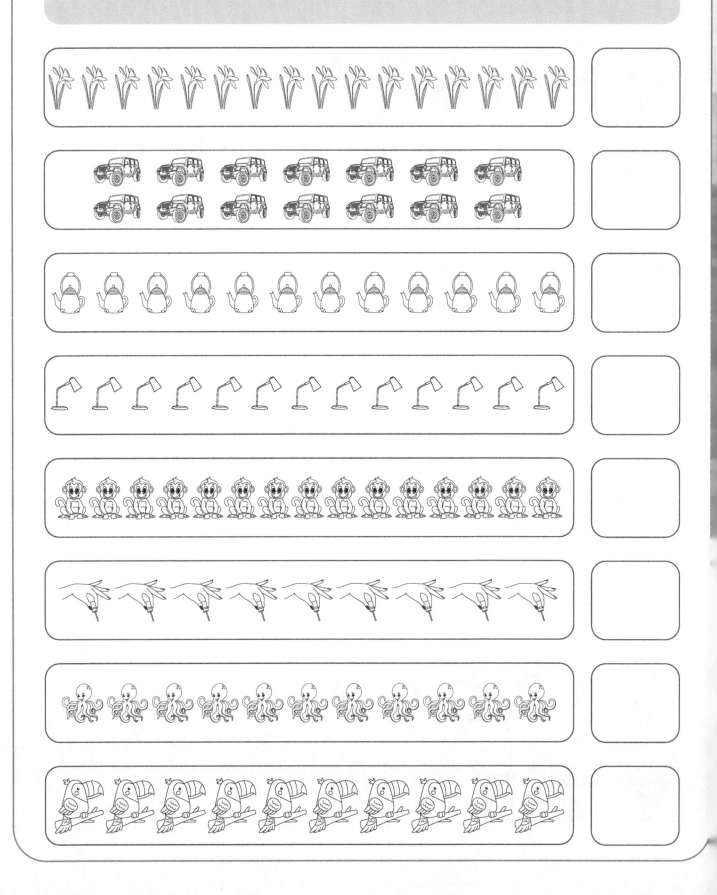

Let's Learn the number Count and Write

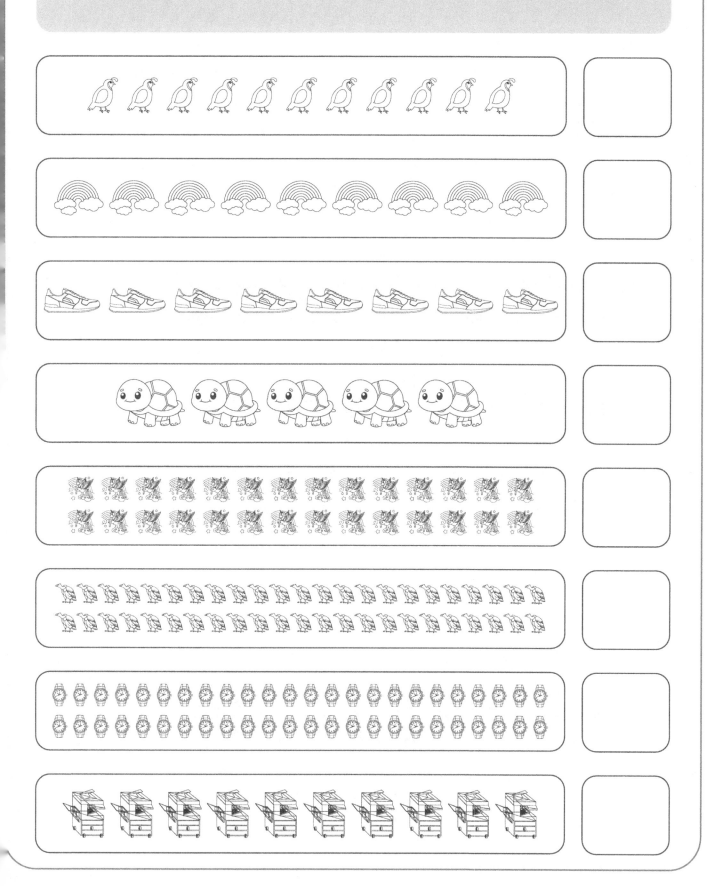

Let's Learn the number Count and Write

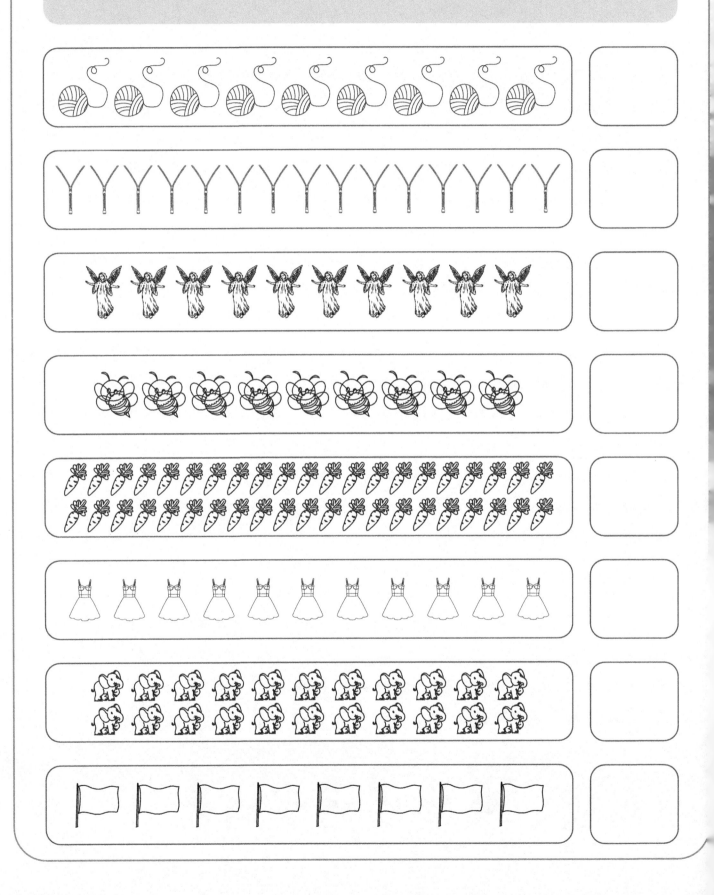

Let's Learn the number Count and Write

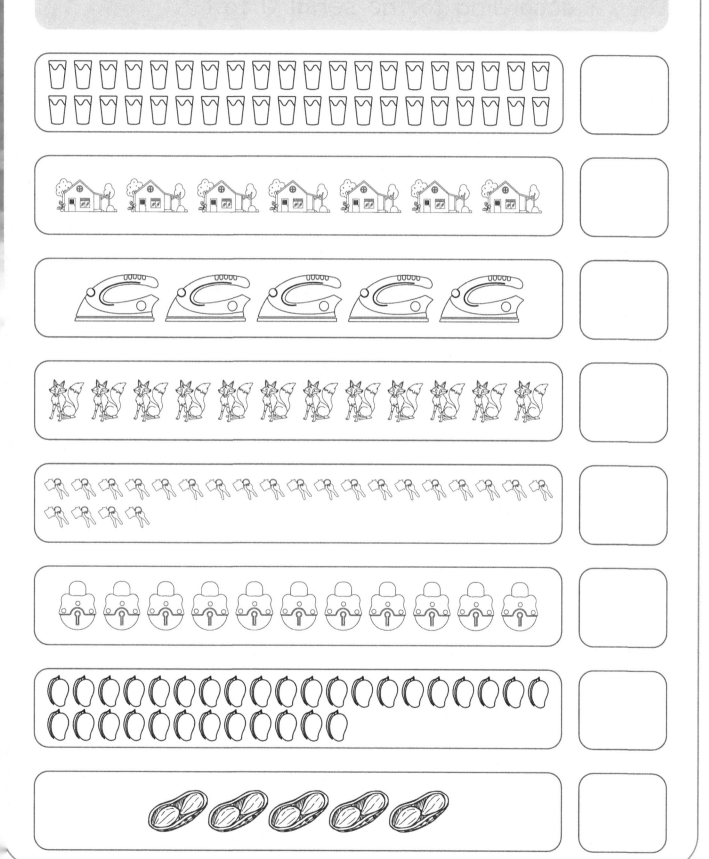

Put the correct number in the box according to the serial (1 to 8)

9	6	1	7	4	
8	2	5	8	2	
3	9	8	9	5	
2	4	6	8	7	
9	6	5	7	4	
7	8	3	6	5	
6	9	5	2	7	
5	8	7	9	8	

Put the correct number in the box according to the serial (9 to 16)

9	7	15	16	14	

12	10	15	15	12	

11	15	11	9	10	

10	12	14	12	16	

15	9	10	12	13	

16	15	11	14	15	

9	10	15	12	14	

10	16	12	16	15	

Put the correct number in the box according to the serial (17 to 24)

2	9	17	8	7	
15	18	12	11	9	
19	10	20	2	4	
6	20	8	10	12	
14	16	21	8	9	
25	28	9	22	5	
6	9	5	23	7	
8	10	12	9	24	

Put the correct number in the box according to the serial (25 to32)

20	6	5	7	25	
8	23	9	26	2	
25	9	27	9	5	
2	28	6	18	7	
29	22	5	25	4	
7	30	3	28	5	
19	9	31	2	7	
5	21	7	32	8	

32	20	1	14	33	
8	2	21	30	34	
3	22	8	35	5	
28	4	6	8	36	
9	25	17	37	4	
24	19	3	6	38	
6	15	5	39	7	
5	27	18	9	40	

Put the correct number in the box according to the serial (41 to 48)

41	28	27	20	25	
25	42	29	38	25	
18	14	43	12	5	
25	17	6	44	21	
21	25	27	17	45	
14	10	13	16	46	
11	9	5	12	47	
14	7	15	28	48	

10	49	11	7	5	
9	50	12	8	18	
8	51	5	19	5	
12	52	16	8	7	
9	16	53	7	25	
17	8	40	54	5	
24	27	5	40	55	
5	8	7	9	56	

Put the correct number in the box according to the serial (57 to 64)

57	6	33	7	4	

8	58	5	45	2	

3	9	59	9	20	

20	4	37	60	7	

9	30	25	7	61	

60	8	51	6	62	

10	9	50	2	63	

28	8	37	9	64	

Fill in the missing numbers (1 to 20)

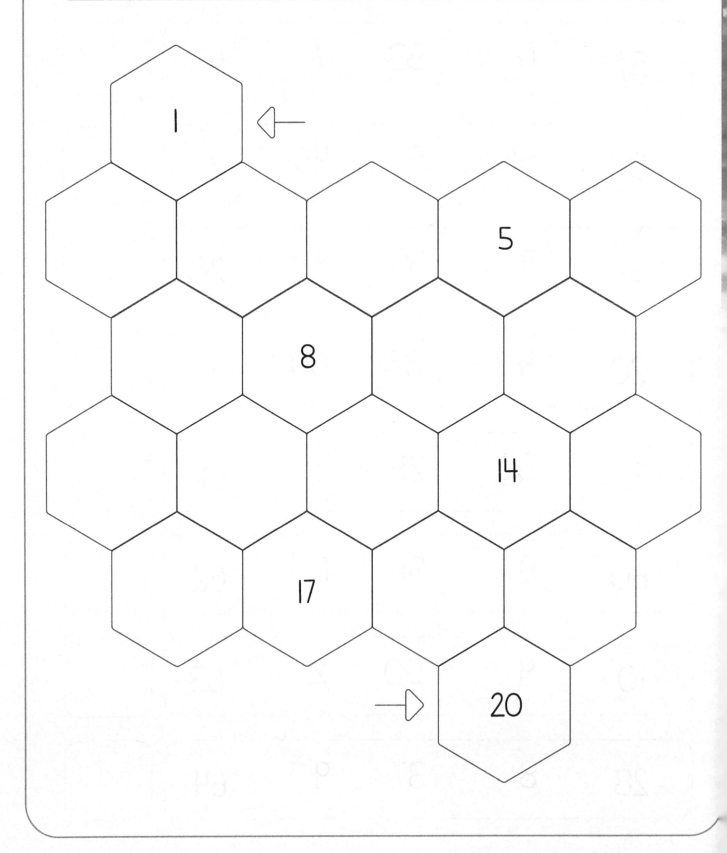

Fill in the missing numbers (21 to 40)

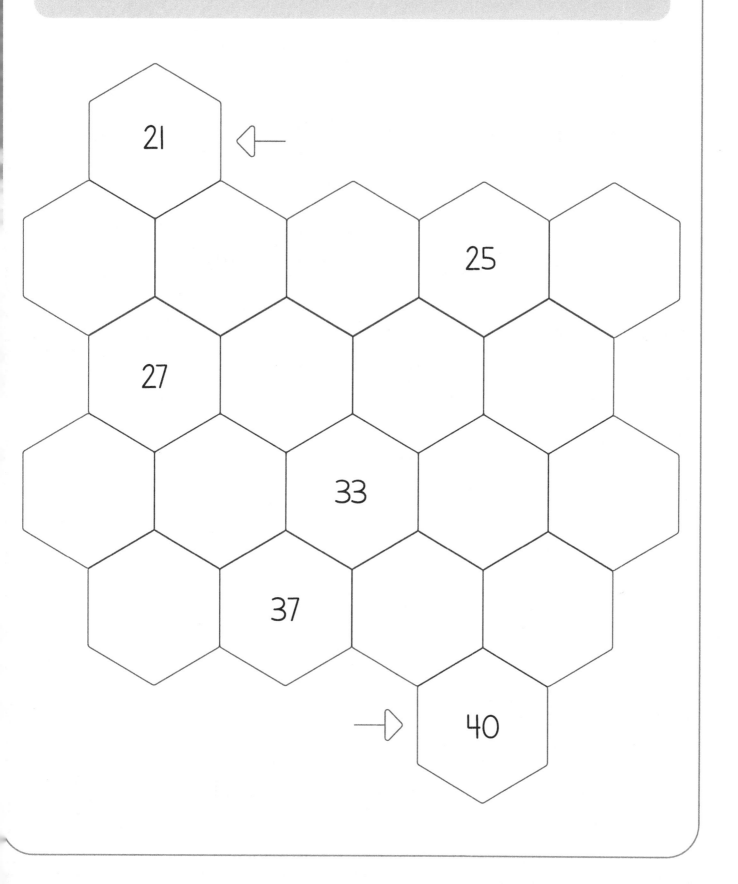

Fill in the missing numbers (41 to 60)

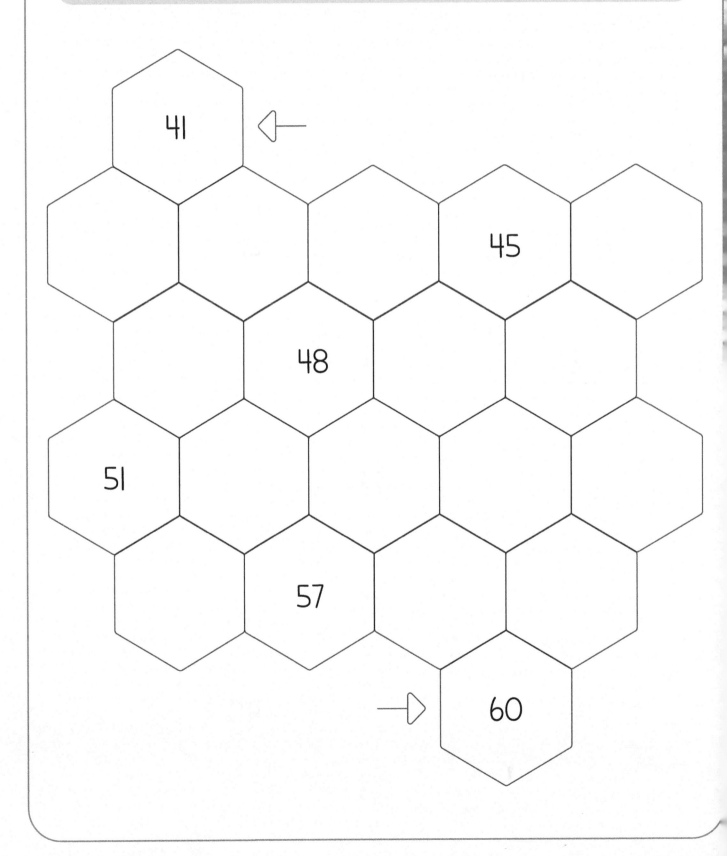

Fill in the missing numbers (61 to 80)

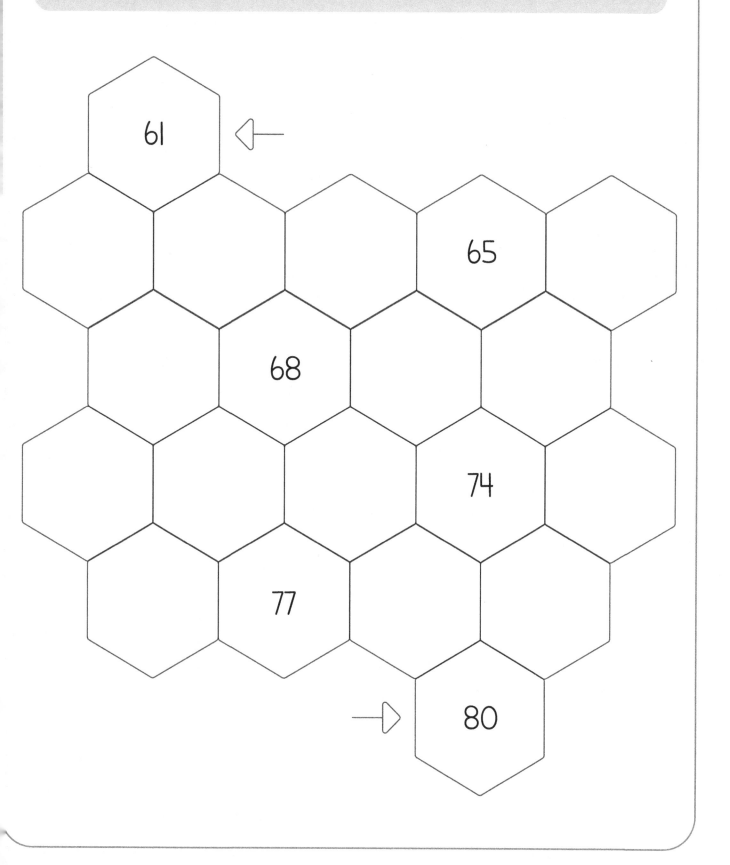

Fill in the missing numbers (81 to 100)

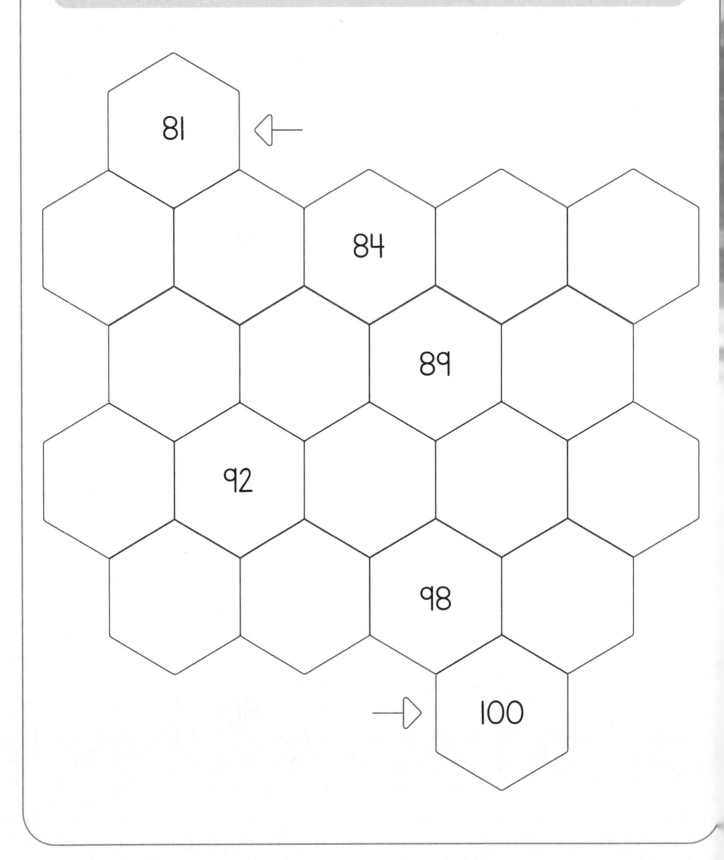

Number maze (1 to 10)

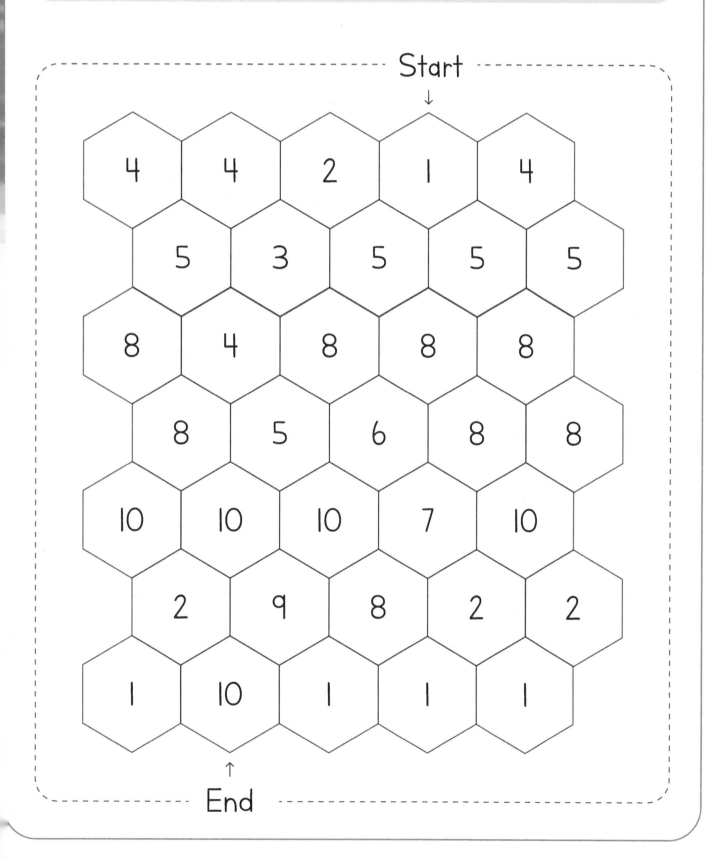

Number maze (11 to 20)

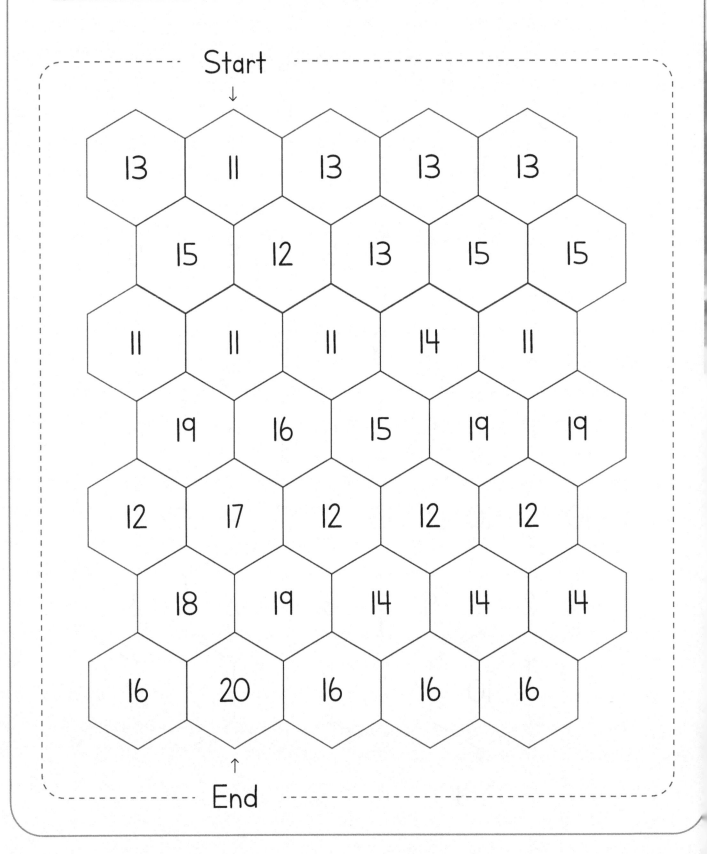

Start

13 11 13 13 13

15 12 13 15 15

11 11 11 14 11

19 16 15 19 19

12 17 12 12 12

18 19 14 14 14

16 20 16 16 16

End

Number maze (21 to 30)

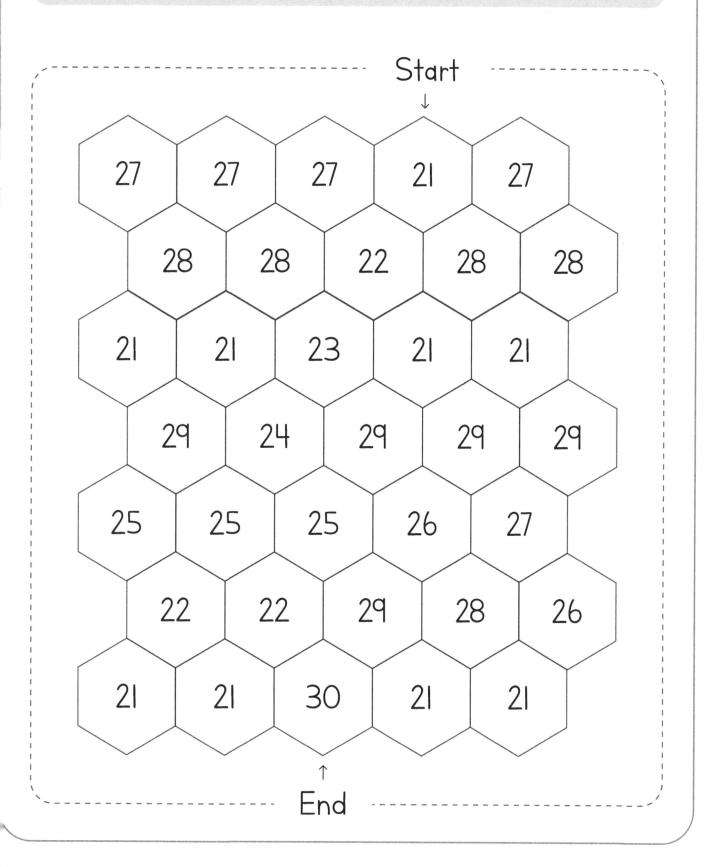

Number maze (31 to 40)

Start
↓

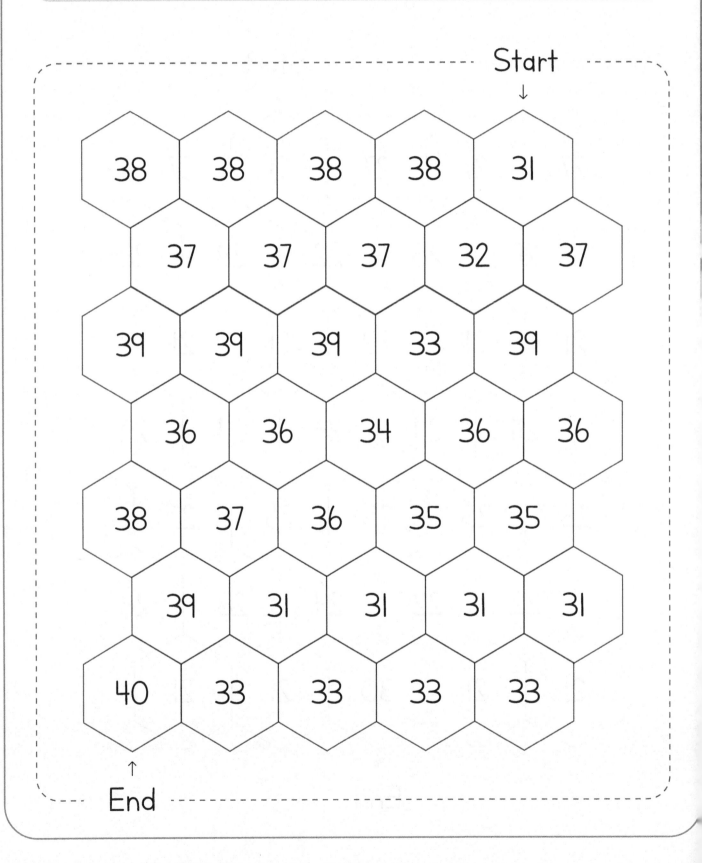

38	38	38	38	31
37	37	37	32	37
39	39	39	33	39
36	36	34	36	36
38	37	36	35	35
39	31	31	31	31
40	33	33	33	33

↑
End

Number maze (41 to 50)

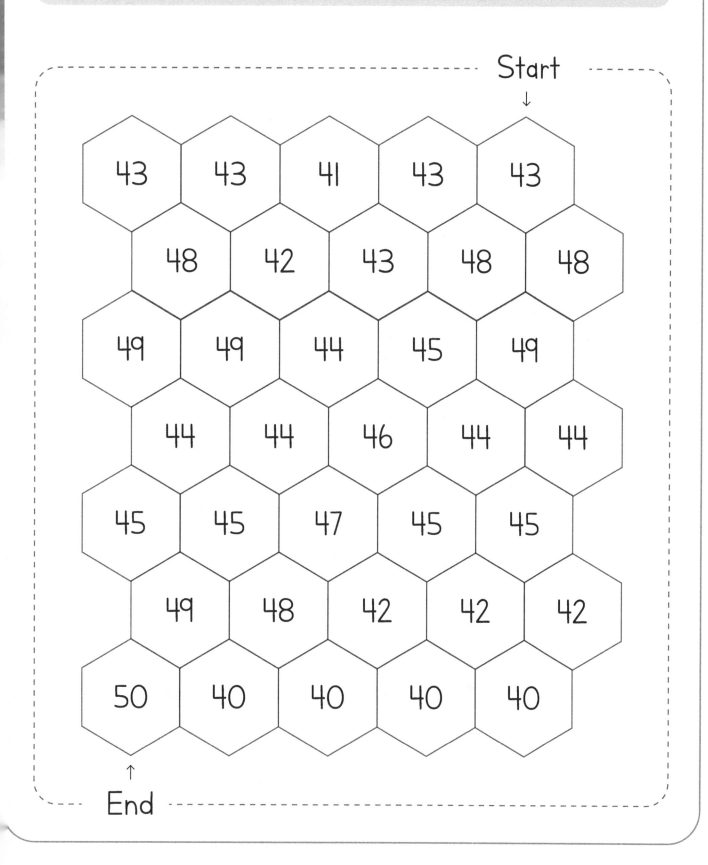

Start
↓

| 43 | 43 | 41 | 43 | 43 |

| 48 | 42 | 43 | 48 | 48 |

| 49 | 49 | 44 | 45 | 49 |

| 44 | 44 | 46 | 44 | 44 |

| 45 | 45 | 47 | 45 | 45 |

| 49 | 48 | 42 | 42 | 42 |

| 50 | 40 | 40 | 40 | 40 |

↑
End

Number maze (51 to 60)

Start
↓

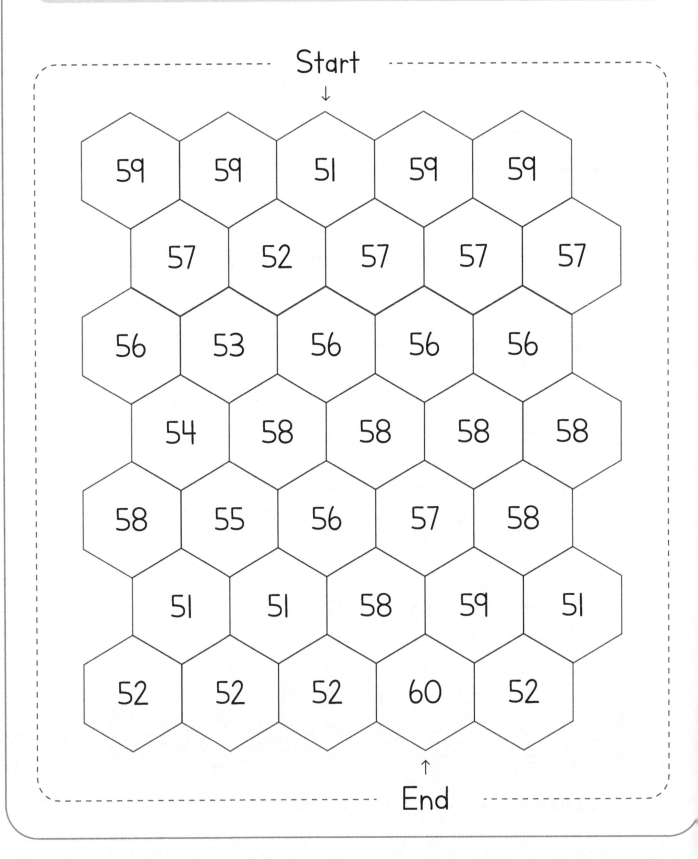

59	59	51	59	59
57	52	57	57	57
56	53	56	56	56
54	58	58	58	58
58	55	56	57	58
51	51	58	59	51
52	52	52	60	52

↑
End

Number maze (61 to 70)

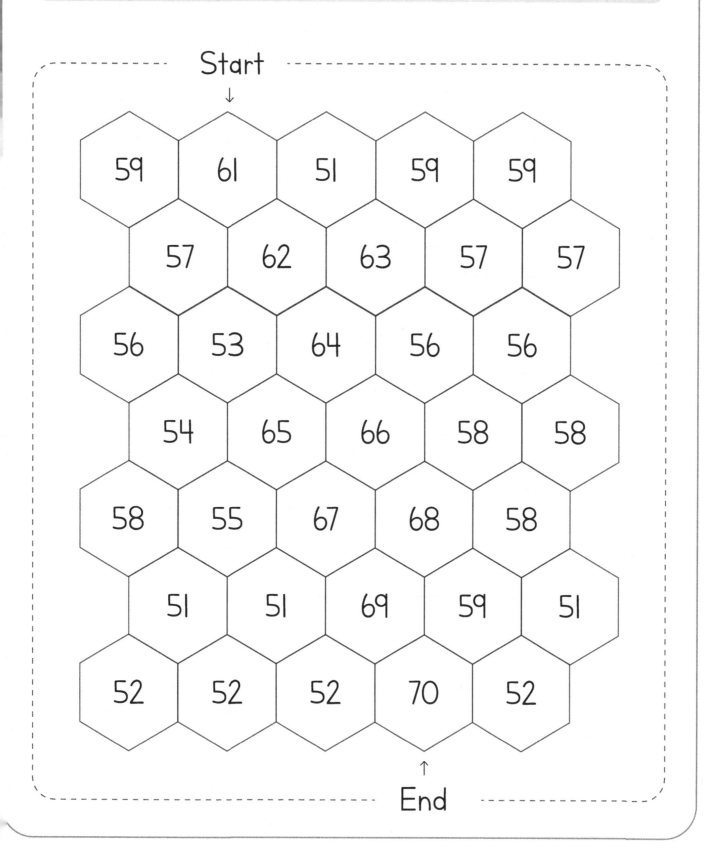

Start ↓

| 59 | 61 | 51 | 59 | 59 |

| 57 | 62 | 63 | 57 | 57 |

| 56 | 53 | 64 | 56 | 56 |

| 54 | 65 | 66 | 58 | 58 |

| 58 | 55 | 67 | 68 | 58 |

| 51 | 51 | 69 | 59 | 51 |

| 52 | 52 | 52 | 70 | 52 |

↑ End

Number maze (71 to 80)

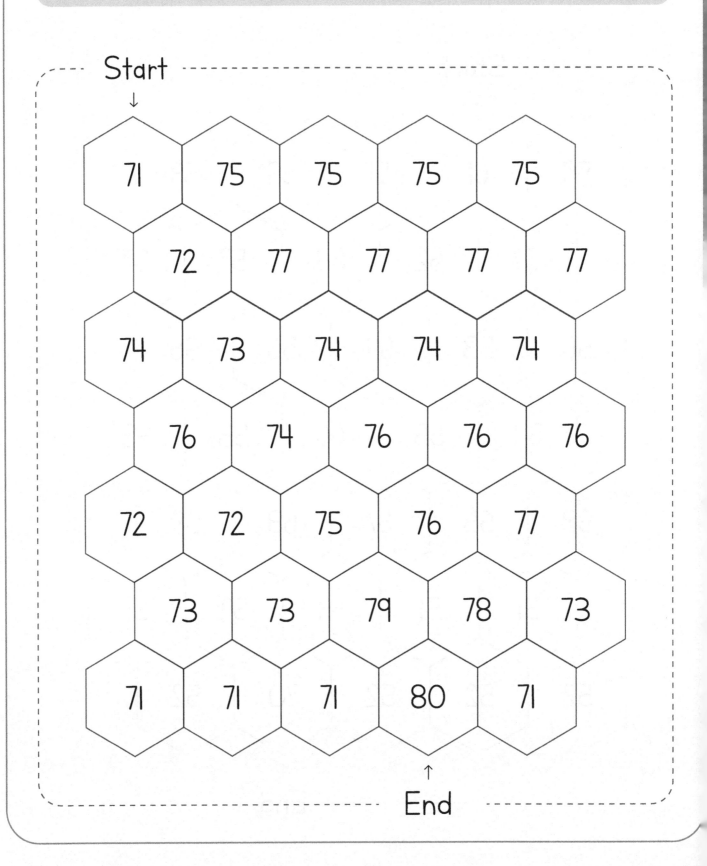

Start

71 75 75 75 75
72 77 77 77 77
74 73 74 74 74
76 74 76 76 76
72 72 75 76 77
73 73 79 78 73
71 71 71 80 71

End

Number maze (81 to 90)

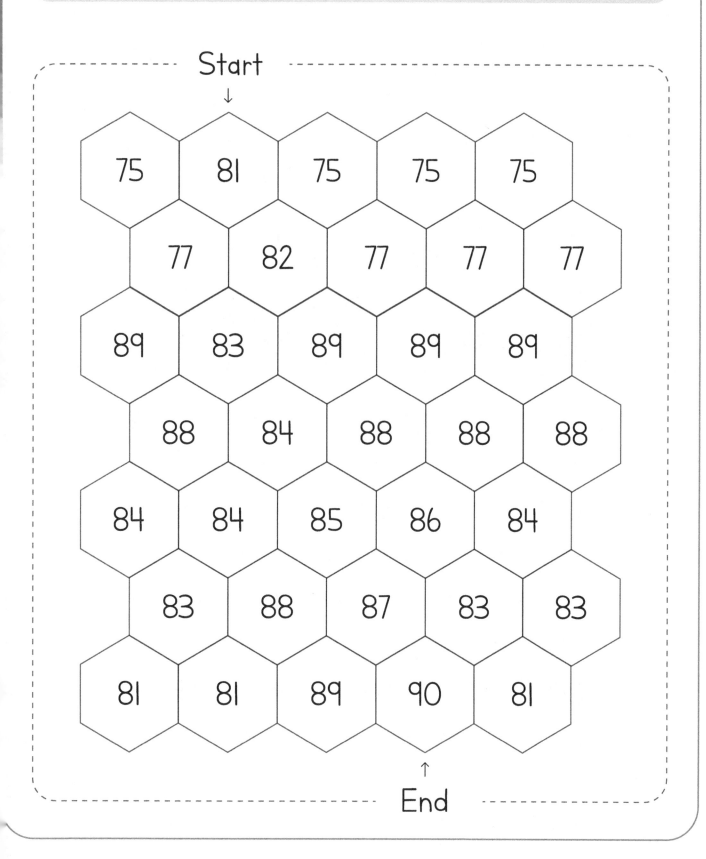

Number maze (91 to 100)

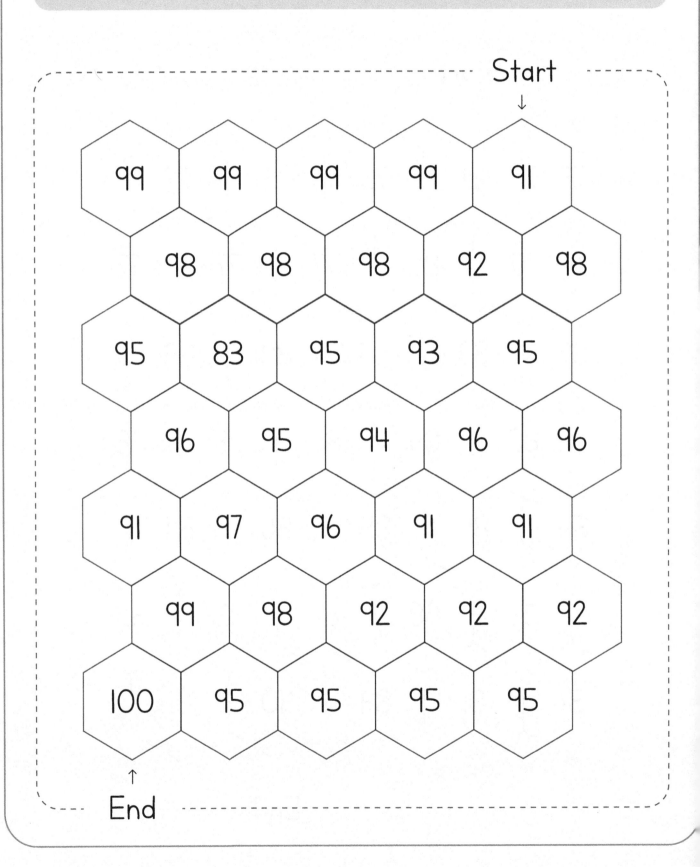

Addition by 1 digit

```
   1          1          1
+  1       +  2       +  3
_____     _____     _____


   1          1          1
+  4       +  5       +  6
_____     _____     _____


   1          1          1
+  7       +  8       +  9
_____     _____     _____


   1          1          1
+  0       + 11       + 12
_____     _____     _____
```

Addition by 2 digit

```
    2          2          2
+  13      +  14      +  15
_____     _____     _____


    2          2          2
+  16      +  17      +  18
_____     _____     _____


    2          2          2
+  19      +  19      +  19
_____     _____     _____


    2          2          2
+  20      +  21      +  22
_____     _____     _____
```

Addition by 3 digit

$$\begin{array}{r} 3 \\ + 23 \\ \hline \end{array}$$
$$\begin{array}{r} 3 \\ + 24 \\ \hline \end{array}$$
$$\begin{array}{r} 3 \\ + 25 \\ \hline \end{array}$$

$$\begin{array}{r} 3 \\ + 26 \\ \hline \end{array}$$
$$\begin{array}{r} 3 \\ + 27 \\ \hline \end{array}$$
$$\begin{array}{r} 3 \\ + 28 \\ \hline \end{array}$$

$$\begin{array}{r} 3 \\ + 29 \\ \hline \end{array}$$
$$\begin{array}{r} 3 \\ + 30 \\ \hline \end{array}$$
$$\begin{array}{r} 3 \\ + 31 \\ \hline \end{array}$$

$$\begin{array}{r} 3 \\ + 32 \\ \hline \end{array}$$
$$\begin{array}{r} 3 \\ + 33 \\ \hline \end{array}$$
$$\begin{array}{r} 3 \\ + 34 \\ \hline \end{array}$$

Addition by 4 digit

```
    4          4          4
+ 3 5      + 3 6      + 3 7
_____     _____     _____


    4          4          4
+ 3 8      + 3 9      + 4 0
_____     _____     _____


    4          4          4
+ 4 1      + 4 2      + 4 3
_____     _____     _____


    4          4          4
+ 4 4      + 4 5      + 4 6
_____     _____     _____
```

Addition by 5 digit

```
    5              5              5
+  47          +  48          +  49
_____         _____         _____


    5              5              5
+  50          +   1          +   2
_____         _____         _____


    5              5              5
+   3          +   4          +   5
_____         _____         _____


    5              5              5
+   6          +   7          +   8
_____         _____         _____
```

Addition by 6 digit

6 + 9	6 + 10	6 + 11
6 + 12	6 + 13	6 + 14
6 + 15	6 + 16	6 + 17
6 + 18	6 + 19	6 + 20

Addition by 7 digit

```
    7           7           7
+  21       + 22       + 23
_____      _____      _____


    7           7           7
+ 24        + 25        + 26
_____      _____      _____


    7           7           7
+ 27        + 28        + 29
_____      _____      _____


    7           7           7
+ 30        + 31        + 32
_____      _____      _____
```

Addition by 8 digit

```
    8              8              8
+  3 3         +  3 4         +  3 5
_____         _____         _____


    8              8              8
+  3 6         +  3 5         +  3 6
_____         _____         _____


    8              8              8
+  3 7         +  3 8         +  3 9
_____         _____         _____


    8              8              8
+  4 0         +  4 1         +  4 2
_____         _____         _____
```

Addition by 9 digit

```
    9            9            9
+  4 3       +  4 4       +  4 5
_____      _____      _____


    9            9            9
+  4 6       +  4 7       +  4 8
_____      _____      _____


    9            9            9
+  4 9       +  5 0       +  1
_____      _____      _____


    9            9            9
+  2         +  3         +  4
_____      _____      _____
```

Addition by 10 digit

$$\begin{array}{r} 10 \\ +\ 5 \\ \hline \end{array}$$

$$\begin{array}{r} 10 \\ +\ 6 \\ \hline \end{array}$$

$$\begin{array}{r} 10 \\ +\ 7 \\ \hline \end{array}$$

$$\begin{array}{r} 10 \\ +\ 8 \\ \hline \end{array}$$

$$\begin{array}{r} 10 \\ +\ 9 \\ \hline \end{array}$$

$$\begin{array}{r} 10 \\ +\ 10 \\ \hline \end{array}$$

$$\begin{array}{r} 10 \\ +\ 11 \\ \hline \end{array}$$

$$\begin{array}{r} 10 \\ +\ 12 \\ \hline \end{array}$$

$$\begin{array}{r} 10 \\ +\ 13 \\ \hline \end{array}$$

$$\begin{array}{r} 10 \\ +\ 14 \\ \hline \end{array}$$

$$\begin{array}{r} 10 \\ +\ 15 \\ \hline \end{array}$$

$$\begin{array}{r} 10 \\ +\ 16 \\ \hline \end{array}$$

Addition by 11 digit

```
   11          11          11
+  17       +  18       +  19
_____      _____      _____


   11          11          11
+  20       +  21       +  22
_____      _____      _____


   11          11          11
+  23       +  24       +  25
_____      _____      _____


   11          11          11
+  26       +  27       +  28
_____      _____      _____
```

```
   12          12          12
+  29       +  30       +  31
_____    _____    _____


   12          12          12
+  32       +  33       +  34
_____    _____    _____


   12          12          12
+  35       +  36       +  37
_____    _____    _____


   12          12          12
+  38       +  39       +  40
_____    _____    _____
```

Addition by 13 digit

```
  13          13          13
+ 41        + 42        + 43
————        ————        ————


  13          13          13
+ 44        + 45        + 46
————        ————        ————


  13          13          13
+ 47        + 48        + 49
————        ————        ————


  13          13          13
+ 50        +  1        +  2
————        ————        ————
```

Addition by 14 digit

```
  14        14        14
+  3      +  4      +  5
----      ----      ----


  14        14        14
+  6      +  7      +  8
----      ----      ----


  14        14        14
+  9      + 10      + 11
----      ----      ----


  14        14        14
+ 12      + 13      + 14
----      ----      ----
```

Addition by 15 digit

```
   15          15          15
+  15       +  16       +  17
------      ------      ------


   15          15          15
+  18       +  19       +  20
------      ------      ------


   15          15          15
+  21       +  22       +  23
------      ------      ------


   15          15          15
+  24       +  25       +  26
------      ------      ------
```

Addition by 16 digit

16 + 27	16 + 28	16 + 29
16 + 30	16 + 31	16 + 32
16 + 33	16 + 34	16 + 35
16 + 36	16 + 37	16 + 38

Addition by 17 digit

```
   17          17          17
+  39       +  40       +  41
_____      _____      _____


   17          17          17
+  42       +  43       +  44
_____      _____      _____


   17          17          17
+  45       +  46       +  47
_____      _____      _____


   17          17          17
+  48       +  49       +  50
_____      _____      _____
```

Addition by 18 digit

18 + 1	18 + 2	18 + 3
18 + 4	18 + 5	18 + 6
18 + 7	18 + 8	18 + 9
18 + 0	18 + 11	18 + 12

Addition by 19 digit

```
   1 9        1 9        1 9
 + 1 3      + 1 4      + 1 5
 _____     _____     _____
```

```
   1 9        1 9        1 9
 + 1 6      + 1 7      + 1 8
 _____     _____     _____
```

```
   1 9        1 9        1 9
 + 1 9      + 2 0      +   0
 _____     _____     _____
```

```
   1 9        1 9        1 9
 + 2 1      + 2 2      + 2 3
 _____     _____     _____
```

Addition by 20 digit

$$
\begin{array}{r} 20 \\ +\ 24 \\ \hline \end{array}
\qquad
\begin{array}{r} 20 \\ +\ 25 \\ \hline \end{array}
\qquad
\begin{array}{r} 20 \\ +\ \ 0 \\ \hline \end{array}
$$

$$
\begin{array}{r} 20 \\ +\ 10 \\ \hline \end{array}
\qquad
\begin{array}{r} 20 \\ +\ 00 \\ \hline \end{array}
\qquad
\begin{array}{r} 20 \\ +\ 70 \\ \hline \end{array}
$$

$$
\begin{array}{r} 20 \\ +\ \ 8 \\ \hline \end{array}
\qquad
\begin{array}{r} 20 \\ +\ \ 9 \\ \hline \end{array}
\qquad
\begin{array}{r} 20 \\ +\ 20 \\ \hline \end{array}
$$

$$
\begin{array}{r} 20 \\ +\ 75 \\ \hline \end{array}
\qquad
\begin{array}{r} 20 \\ +\ 85 \\ \hline \end{array}
\qquad
\begin{array}{r} 20 \\ +\ 80 \\ \hline \end{array}
$$

Addition Worksheet Matching

3 axes + 2 axes ★ 6

5 hammers + 5 hammers ★ 4

2 birds + 2 birds ★ 5

2 lamps + 1 lamp ★ 10

3 camels + 3 camels ★ 3

Addition Worksheet Matching

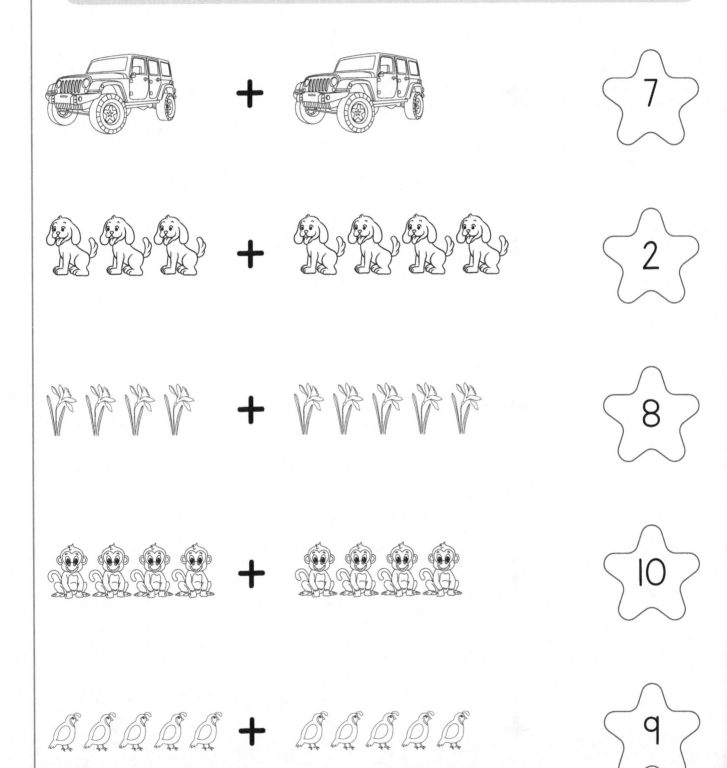

Addition Worksheet Matching

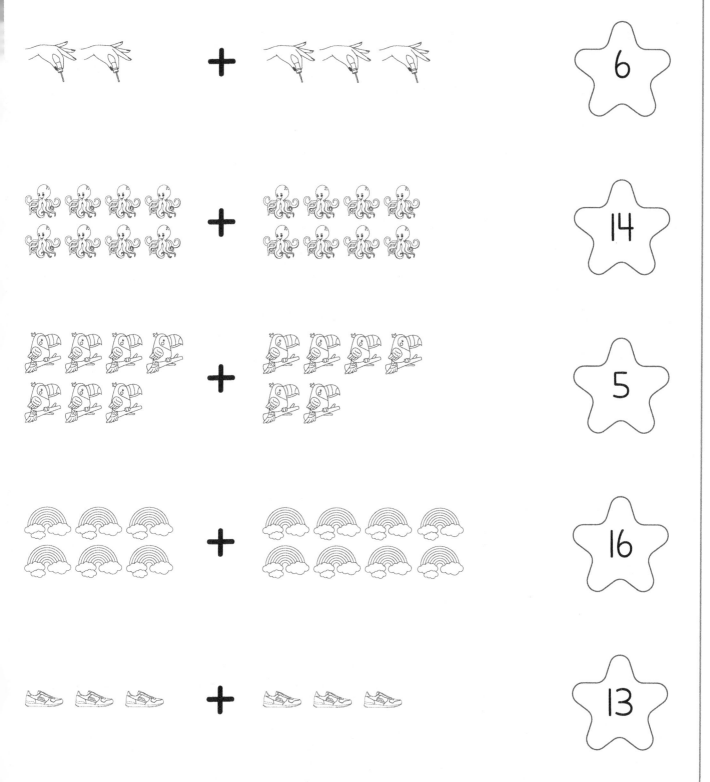

Addition Worksheet Matching

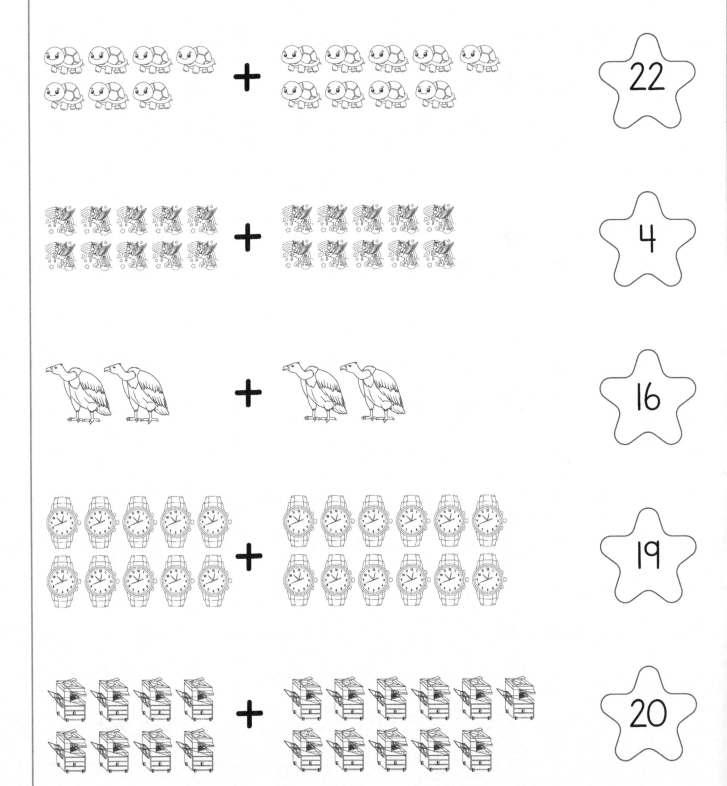

Addition Worksheet Matching

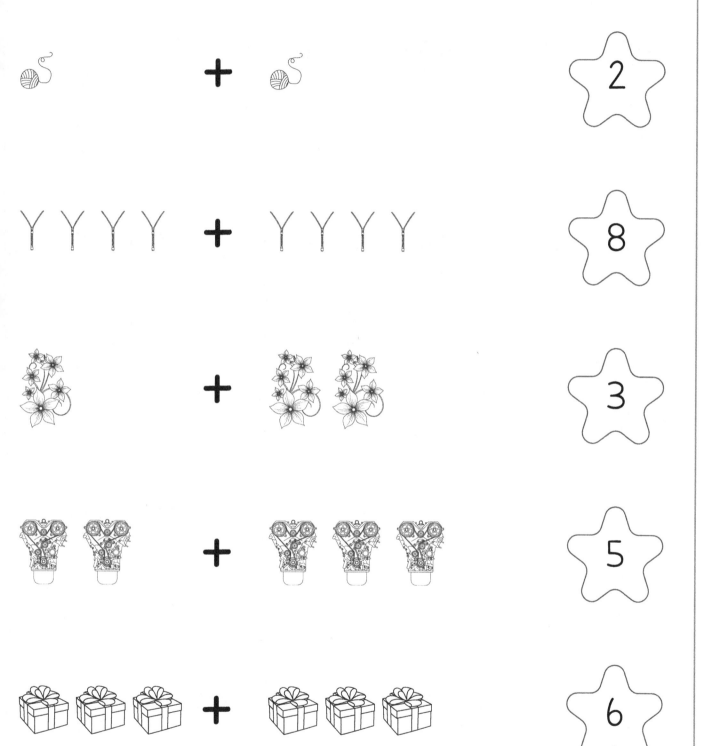

Addition Worksheet Matching

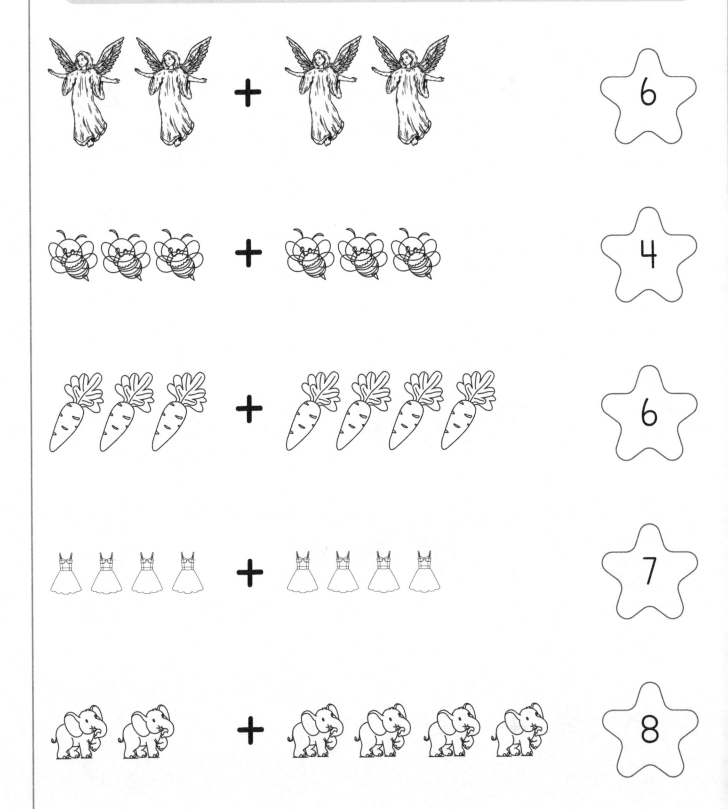

Addition Worksheet Matching

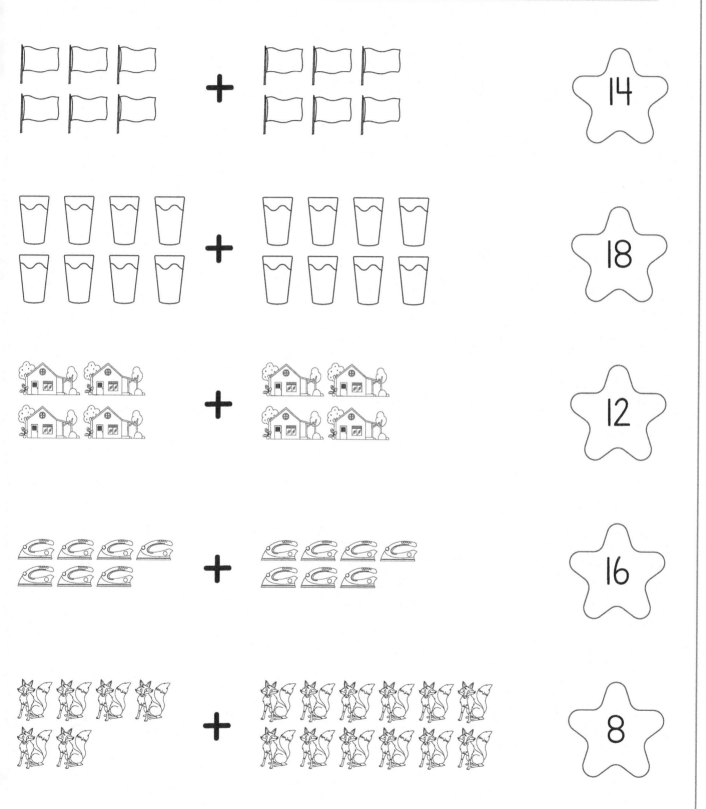

Addition Worksheet Matching

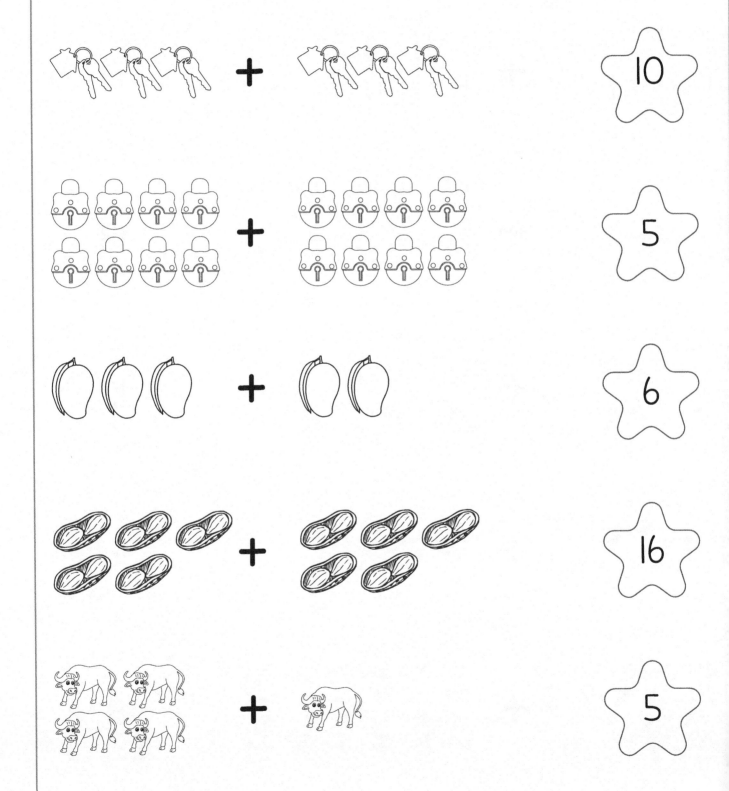

Addition Worksheet Matching

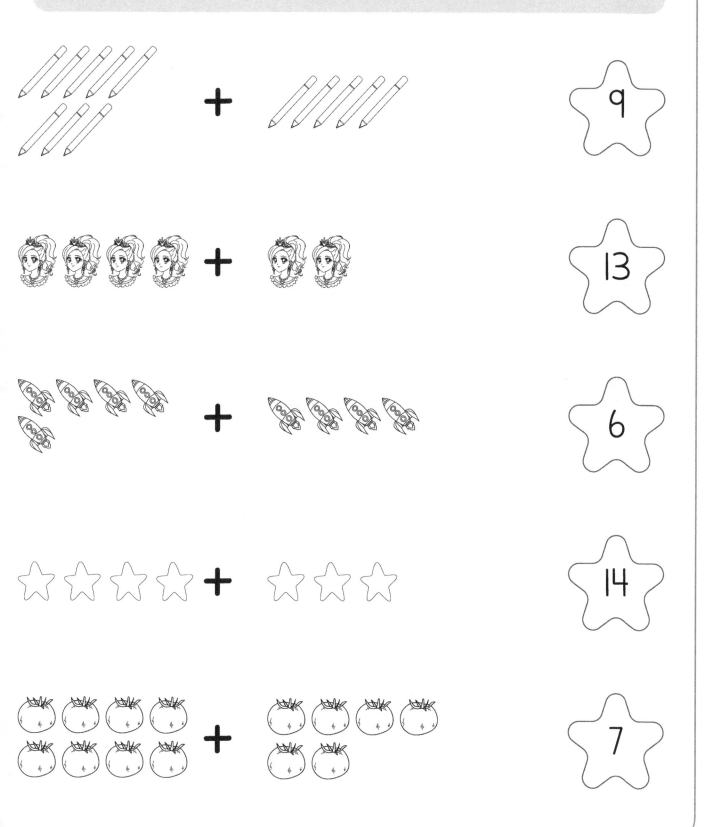

Addition Worksheet Matching

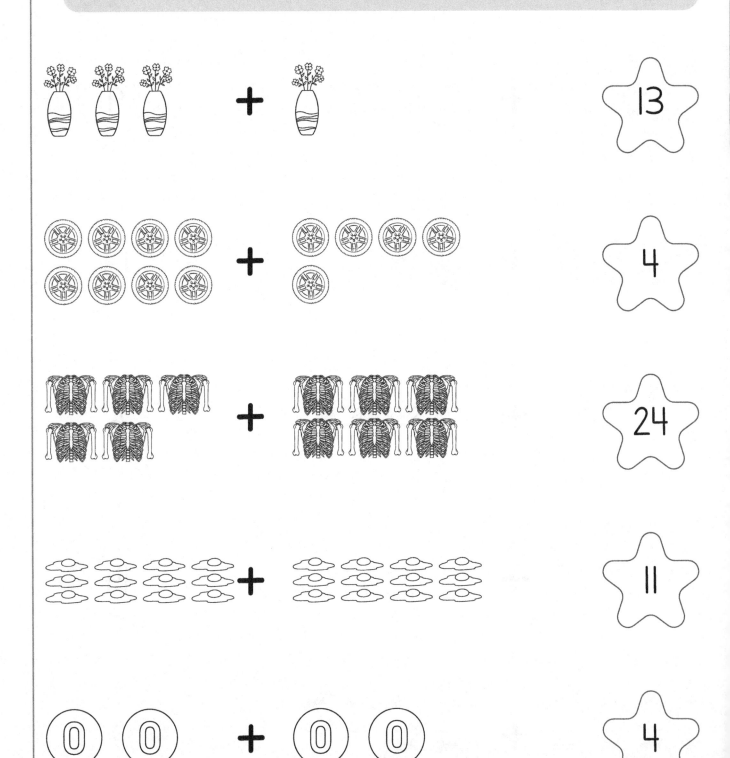

Count and write the number in the box

卌 卌	
卌 卌 |||	
卌 |||	
卌		
卌 卌 卌	

Count and write the number in the box

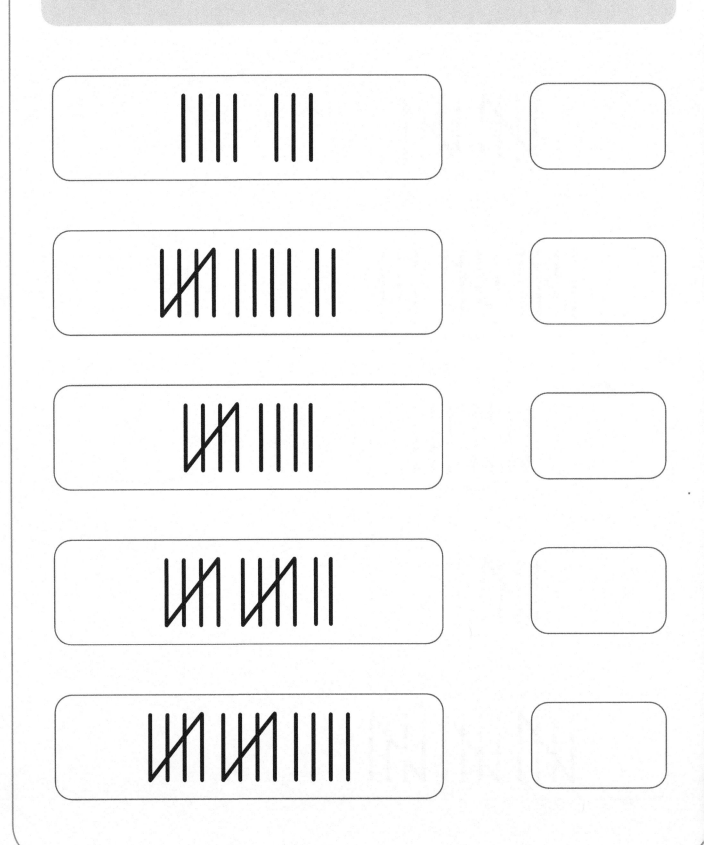

Count and write the number in the box

Tally marks	Number
ЖЖ ЖЖ ЖЖ ЖЖ	
ЖЖ ЖЖ ЖЖ I	
ЖЖ ЖЖ ЖЖ III	
ЖЖ ЖЖ ЖЖ IIII	
ЖЖ ЖЖ ЖЖ II	

Count and write the number in the box

‖‖ ‖‖ ‖‖ ‖‖ ‖‖	
‖‖ ‖‖ ‖‖ ‖‖ ‖‖ I	
‖‖ ‖‖ ‖‖ ‖‖ ‖‖ III	
‖‖ ‖‖ ‖‖ ‖‖ ‖‖ IIII	
‖‖ ‖‖ ‖‖ ‖‖ ‖‖ II	

Count and write the number in the box

####### ||||| ||||| |||

####### ||||| ||||| |||||

####### ||||| ||||| ||||| ||

####### ||||| ||||| ||||| |

####### ||||| |||||

Count and write the number in the box

‖‖ |

‖‖ ‖

‖‖ |||

‖‖ ‖‖ ‖‖

‖‖ ‖‖ ‖‖‖‖

Count and write the number in the box

| | |

[ ]

|||| ||

[ ]

|||| |||||

[ ]

|||| ||||| |||

[ ]

|||| |||| |||||

[ ]

Count and write the number in the box

⑷⑷⑷	
⑷⑷ IIII	
⑷ III	
⑷⑷⑷ I	
⑷⑷ III	

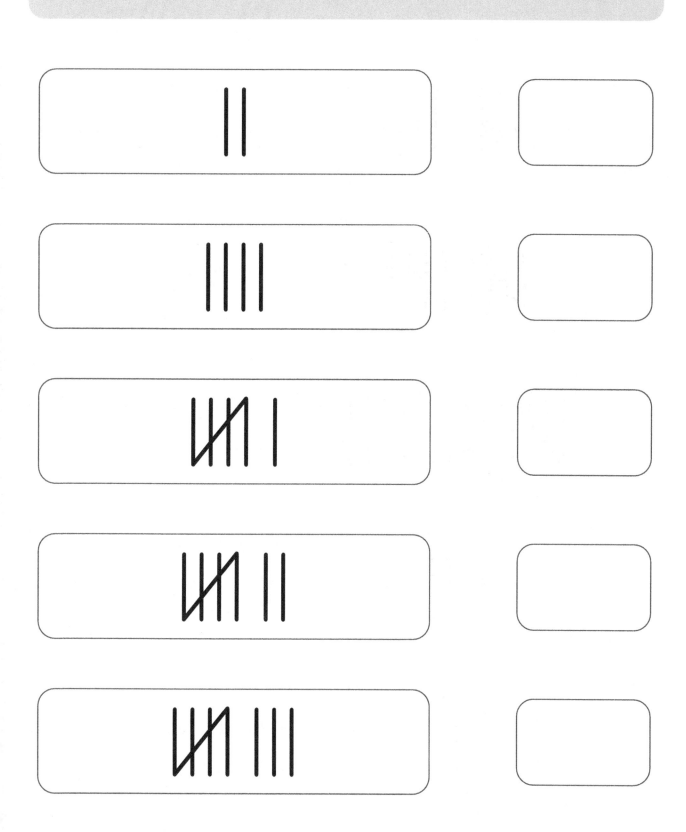

Count and write the number in the box

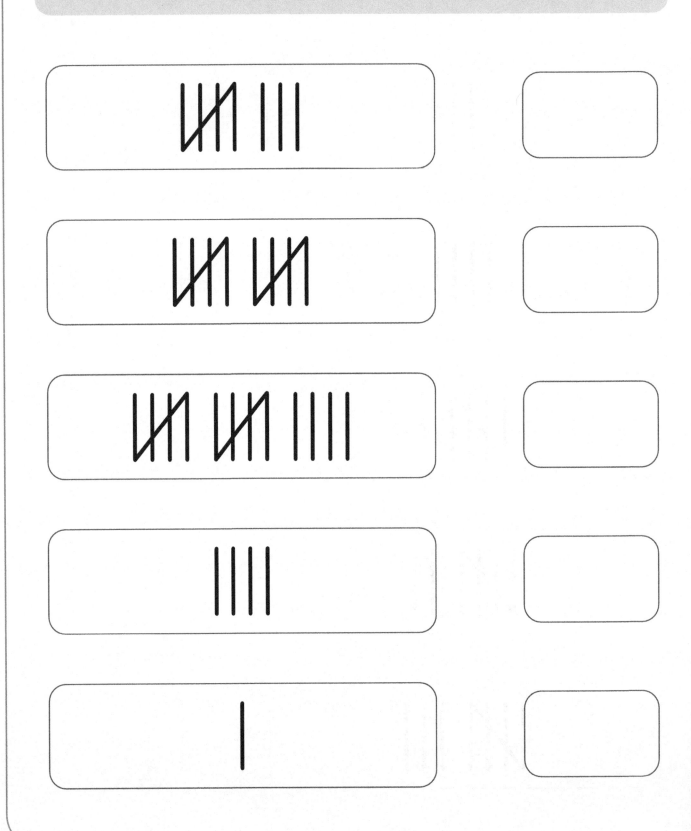

Subtraction (0 to 5)

0 - 0 ———	2 - 1 ———	3 - 2 ———
4 - 2 ———	5 - 1 ———	1 - 0 ———
3 - 1 ———	4 - 1 ———	4 - 3 ———
5 - 2 ———	5 - 3 ———	5 - 4 ———

Subtraction (6 to 10)

6 - 1	6 - 5	9 - 9
9 - 8	8 - 7	6 - 6
8 - 4	9 - 5	7 - 2
10 - 2	10 - 0	9 - 1

Subtraction (11 to 15)

11 − 5	12 − 6	11 − 0
13 − 2	15 − 5	18 − 18
20 − 1	20 − 9	17 − 9
14 − 7	15 − 6	16 − 9

Subtraction (16 to 20)

```
   17          15          20
 -  8        -  6        -  9
 _____      _____      _____


   18          17          16
 -  2        -  9        -  0
 _____      _____      _____


   18          19          17
 -  9        -  5        -  8
 _____      _____      _____


   19          20          16
 - 19        -  0        -  4
 _____      _____      _____
```

Subtraction (21 to 25)

25 - 0	25 - 21	21 - 3
22 - 2	24 - 8	23 - 14
25 - 20	23 - 19	24 - 24
25 - 21	24 - 3	25 - 25

Subtraction (26 to 30)

30	26	28
- 0	- 21	- 25
———	———	———

30	29	27
- 15	- 9	- 25
———	———	———

26	28	30
- 1	- 5	- 8
———	———	———

26	27	30
- 9	- 10	- 4
———	———	———

Subtraction (31 to 35)

```
    31          34          32
  - 15        - 11        -  2
  _____      _____      _____


    33          34          32
  - 33        -  8        -  0
  _____      _____      _____


    35          31          35
  - 31        -  8        -  9
  _____      _____      _____


    31          32          33
  - 10        - 18        - 31
  _____      _____      _____
```

Subtraction (36 to 40)

$$\begin{array}{r} 40 \\ -\ 40 \\ \hline \end{array} \qquad \begin{array}{r} 38 \\ -\ 5 \\ \hline \end{array} \qquad \begin{array}{r} 40 \\ -\ 9 \\ \hline \end{array}$$

$$\begin{array}{r} 39 \\ -\ 0 \\ \hline \end{array} \qquad \begin{array}{r} 36 \\ -\ 8 \\ \hline \end{array} \qquad \begin{array}{r} 39 \\ -\ 25 \\ \hline \end{array}$$

$$\begin{array}{r} 37 \\ -\ 9 \\ \hline \end{array} \qquad \begin{array}{r} 38 \\ -\ 31 \\ \hline \end{array} \qquad \begin{array}{r} 36 \\ -\ 3 \\ \hline \end{array}$$

$$\begin{array}{r} 37 \\ -\ 7 \\ \hline \end{array} \qquad \begin{array}{r} 36 \\ -\ 30 \\ \hline \end{array} \qquad \begin{array}{r} 40 \\ -\ 36 \\ \hline \end{array}$$

Subtraction (41 to 45)

```
    41          45          44
  - 25        -  5        - 12
  _____      _____      _____


    42          45          42
  - 28        - 40        - 13
  _____      _____      _____


    43          42          43
  -  3        - 22        - 41
  _____      _____      _____


    44          43          45
  -  9        - 21        - 45
  _____      _____      _____
```

Subtraction (46 to 50)

46 − 25	48 − 30	47 − 9
49 − 0	50 − 25	49 − 28
47 − 1	48 − 9	50 − 7
50 − 0	46 − 7	48 − 9

Subtraction (51 to 55)

```
    51          53          55
  -  6        -  4        -  9
  _____      _____      _____


    52          53          55
  - 18        - 36        - 50
  _____      _____      _____


    52          53          49
  -  5        -  7        -  0
  _____      _____      _____


    51          55          54
  -  6        -  9        -  8
  _____      _____      _____
```

Subtraction (56 to 60)

57 - 50	57 - 9	58 - 7
57 - 0	59 - 10	58 - 19
58 - 29	57 - 38	59 - 25
56 - 0	56 - 56	60 - 0

Subtraction (61 to 65)

61 − 31	65 − 12	64 − 14
63 − 60	63 − 29	65 − 39
62 − 61	61 − 20	63 − 35
64 − 0	65 − 9	62 − 2

Subtraction (66 to 70)

$$66 - 0$$

$$70 - 10$$

$$67 - 50$$

$$67 - 35$$

$$70 - 50$$

$$66 - 6$$

$$68 - 1$$

$$69 - 9$$

$$69 - 59$$

$$69 - 55$$

$$68 - 17$$

$$70 - 35$$

Subtraction (71 to 75)

```
   71          75          73
 -  1        -  5        -  3
 ____        ____        ____


   72          74          75
 - 12        - 64        - 29
 ____        ____        ____


   71          74          72
 -  9        - 15        - 36
 ____        ____        ____


   73          75          71
 -  9        -  8        - 71
 ____        ____        ____
```

Subtraction (76 to 80)

```
  80          80          79
-  0        - 10        -  9
____        ____        ____


  76          77          78
-  7        -  9        - 66
____        ____        ____


  80          79          76
- 50        - 19        - 70
____        ____        ____


  77          78          80
-  9        - 15        - 75
____        ____        ____
```

Subtraction (81 to 85)

82 − 2	82 − 5	85 − 5
83 − 3	84 − 60	83 − 46
82 − 59	80 − 50	81 − 59
85 − 65	80 − 0	80 − 80

Subtraction (86 to 90)

90	86	86
− 0	− 6	− 80

88	89	89
− 55	− 59	− 79

87	88	88
− 9	− 9	− 77

86	89	90
− 16	− 79	− 90

Subtraction (91 to 95)

91 − 91	92 − 90	92 − 9
93 − 7	95 − 5	91 − 10
92 − 18	93 − 23	94 − 4
95 − 9	95 − 0	92 − 7

Subtraction (96 to 100)

100 - 0	96 - 5	97 - 9
98 - 45	97 - 25	98 - 9
97 - 1	98 - 8	99 - 9
100 - 2	100 - 9	100 - 99

Addition with object

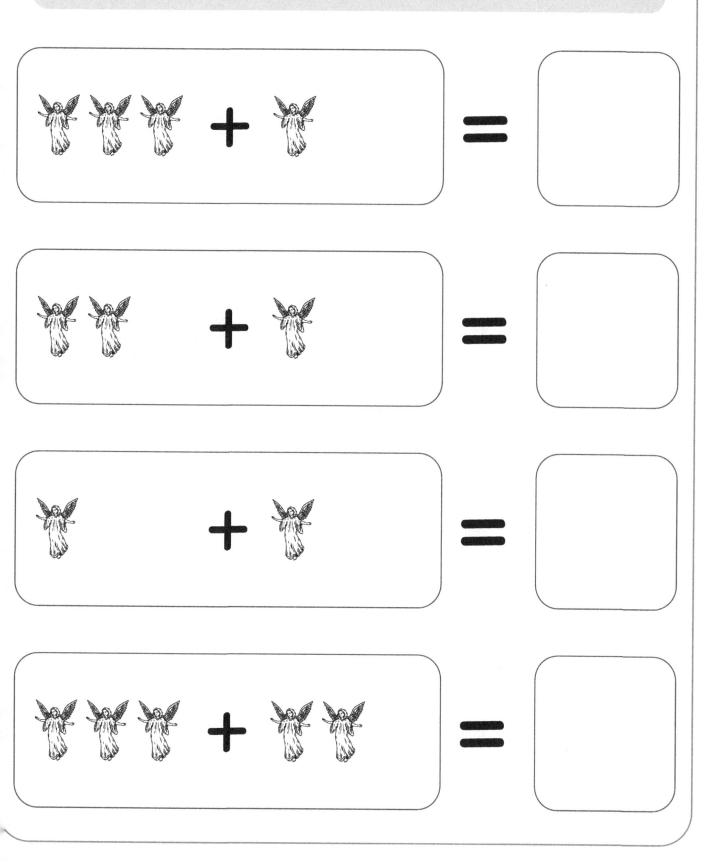

Addition with object

+ =

+ =

+ =

+ =

Addition with object

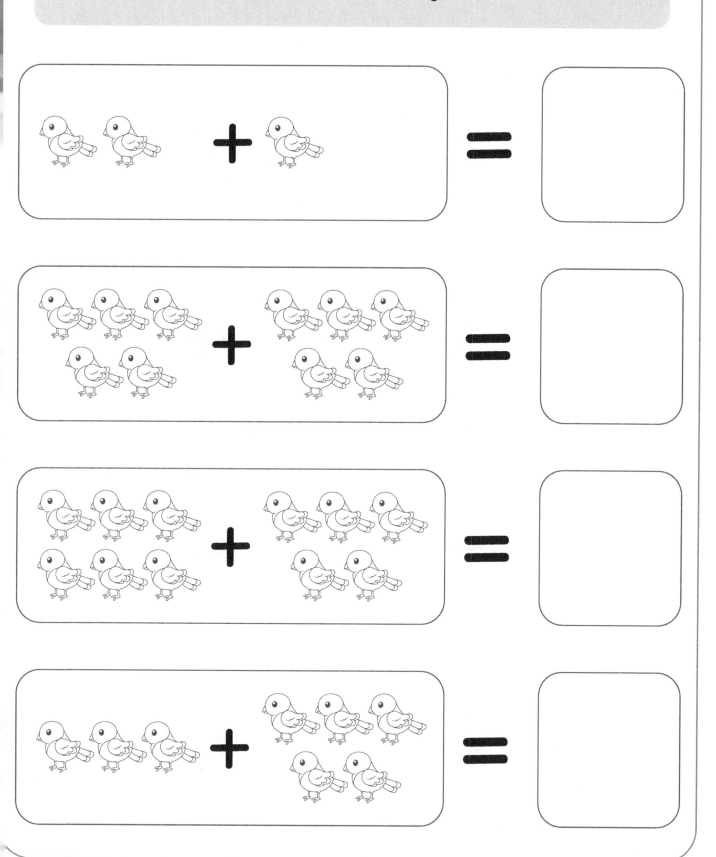

Addition with object

2 + 5 =

5 + 5 =

8 + 8 =

4 + 8 =

Addition with object

+ **=**

+ **=**

+ **=**

+ **=**

Subtraction with object

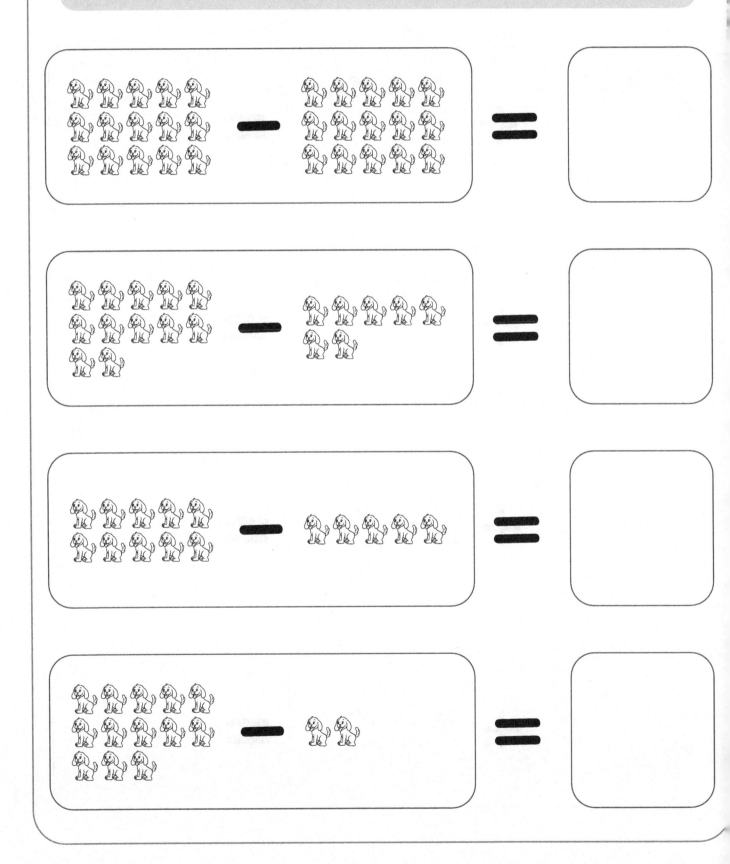

Addition with object

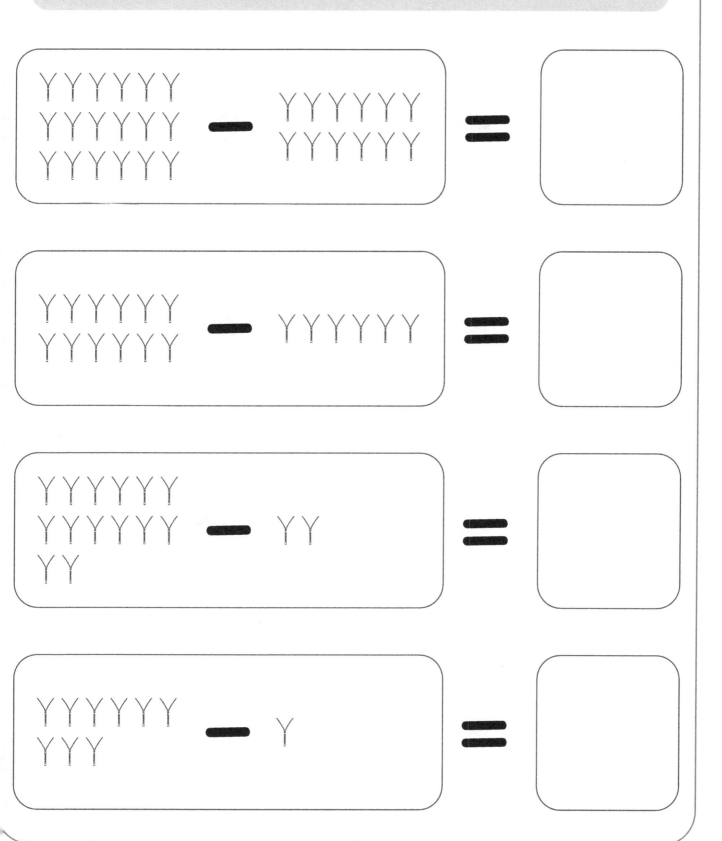

Addition with object

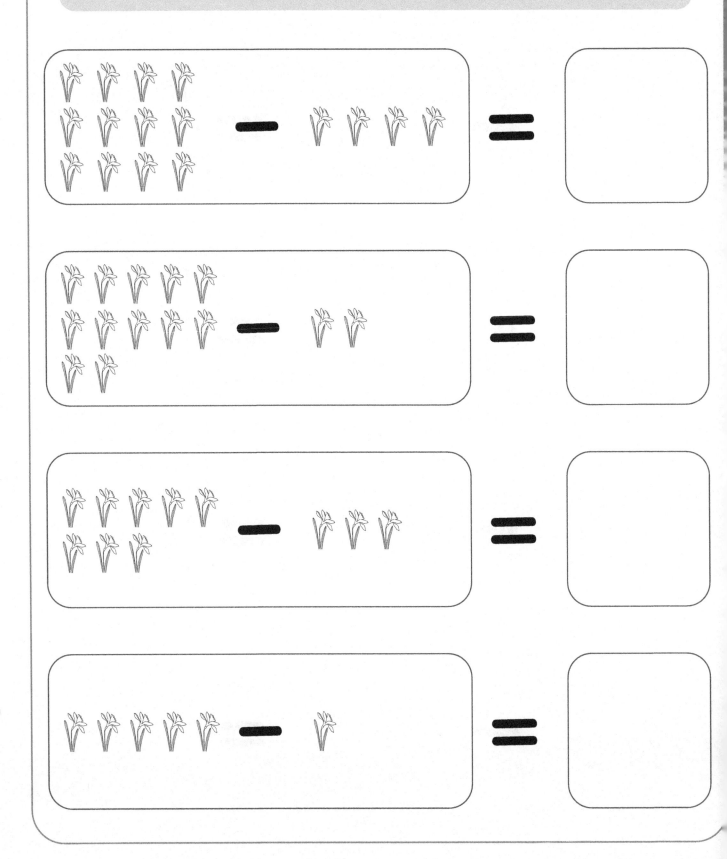

Addition with object

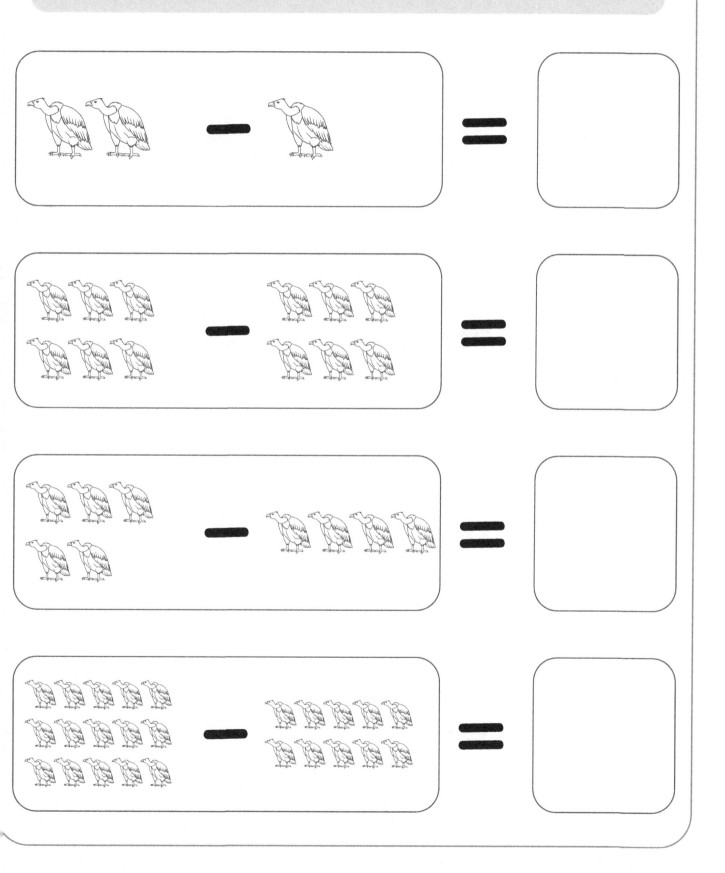

Addition with object

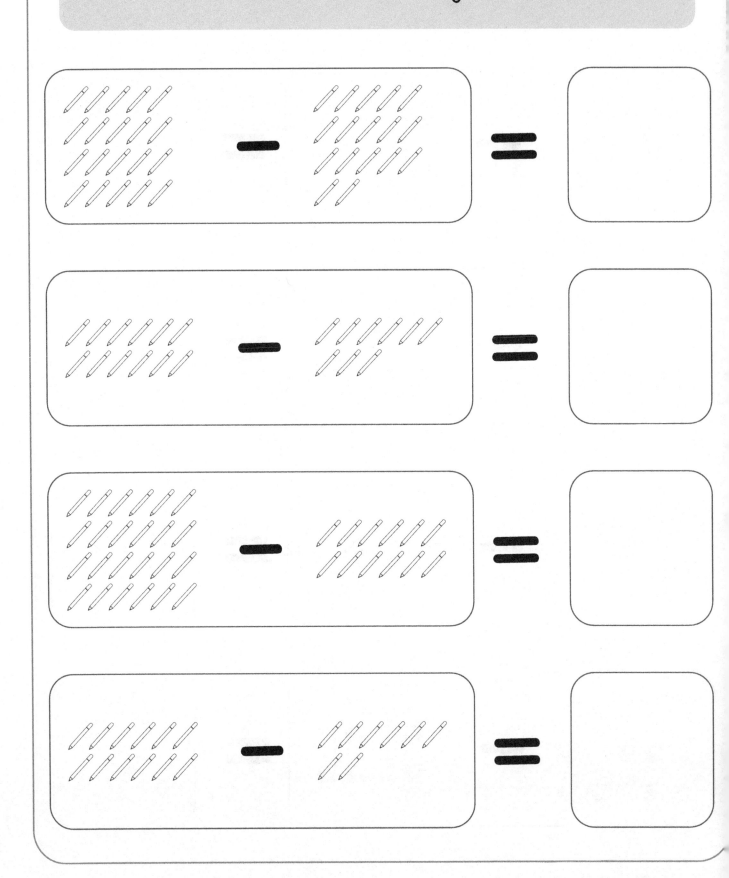

Circle the correct number of pictures

8	4
5	2

9	8
12	4

10	6
9	16

Circle the correct number of pictures

7	3
4	2

14	12
16	18

10	14
16	11

Circle the correct number of pictures

(pictures)	8	4
	3	1
(pictures)	13	11
	20	17
(pictures)	20	18
	12	16

Circle the correct number of pictures

	9	14
	12	10
	5	6
	7	8
	11	13
	15	9

Circle the correct number of pictures

	9	7
	5	8
	11	12
	15	13
	2	4
	6	8

Circle the correct number of pictures

	19	15
	11	18
	8	7
	2	5
	30	28
	25	21

Circle the correct number of pictures

	12	17
	15	20
	14	12
	13	10
	10	12
	15	09

Circle the correct number of pictures

		12	17
		15	20
		10	8
		5	7
		5	6
		8	2

Graph

Made in the USA
Monee, IL
07 June 2024

59567333R00070